CW00867786

SAINT PAUL
FRIEND OF JESUS

JACK O'NEILL

Saint Paul
Friend of Jesus

Illustrations by
Katie Teague

ST PAULS

Published by ST PAULS, UK

Copyright © ST PAULS UK, 2008

ISBN 978-0-85439-748-8

Set by TuKan DTP, Stubbington, Fareham, UK
Printed by AGAM, Cuneo, Italy.

ST PAULS is an activity of the priests and brothers
of the Society of St Paul who proclaim the Gospel
through the media of social communication.

Introduction

The man called Saul was an enemy of Jesus,
but after meeting him he became his friend and
changed his name to Paul.

The rest of Paul's life was spent
telling people about Jesus and helping them
to become his friends as well.

This book tells the story of Saul who became Paul.

Stephen is thrown out of the city

After Jesus died and rose from the dead, his disciples, filled with the Holy Spirit, went everywhere telling people about Jesus. People called them Christians because they believed that Jesus Christ was the Son of God. After listening to the disciples, many people followed them and believed in Jesus.

One of these new Christians was a young man called Stephen. Many of the people in Jerusalem did not like him because he blamed the Jewish people for the death of Jesus.

Finally they became so angry with Stephen that they wanted to kill him and threw him out of the city.

The stoning of Stephen

While they were throwing stones at Stephen they left their coats beside a man named Saul.

Saul was born in the city of Tarsus. As he grew up he tried to live a good life. He studied hard and he became a Pharisee – someone who knows a lot about the story of God and the Jewish people.

When Saul heard that the Christians were saying Jesus was the Son of God he was angry because he thought they were telling lies.

Although he did not throw the stones that killed Stephen, he thought it was a good thing that Stephen was stoned to death.

Saul goes to Damascus

After he watched Stephen being stoned to death, Saul decided that he was going to stop the Christians telling people about Jesus. He went to the High Priest in the temple and offered to help.

He was very good at finding Christians. When he found them he arrested them and sent them to prison. The High Priest gave Saul the job of going to the city of Damascus where many Christians lived.

Saul was going to find them and put them in prison.

The Conversion of Saul

Saul was riding his horse
and was nearly at the city
of Damascus when a bright
light flashed all around
him. His horse reared up,
and when Saul fell to the
ground, he looked around
him but could not see
because the light was so
bright. When he was
on the ground he heard
a voice saying: "Saul, Saul,
why do you persecute me?"

Saul asked the voice: "Who are you?" and the voice replied: "I am Jesus, the one you are persecuting."

The voice of Jesus then told Saul to get up and go to the city of Damascus where he would learn what he had to do.

Saul tried to get up but he realised that he was blind. The people he was travelling with had to lead him to Damascus where he sat and waited for three days.

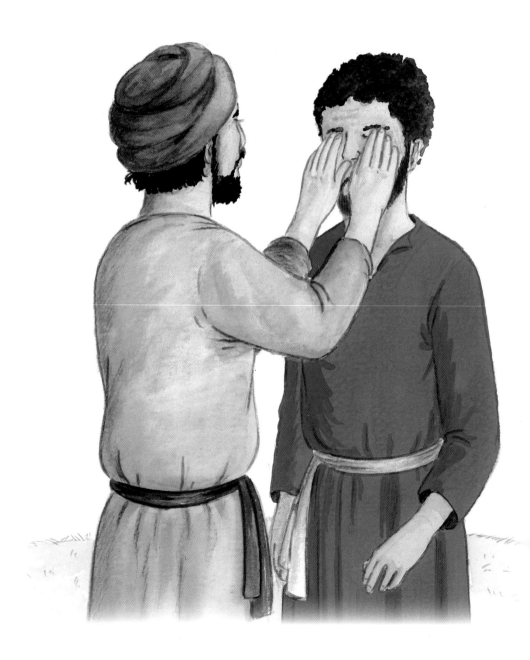

Saul becomes Paul

 In the city of Damascus there lived a Christian called Ananias. Jesus appeared to him in a vision and told him to go to Saul.

Ananias was frightened because he had heard that Saul persecuted Christians, but Jesus said that he wanted Saul to become a Christian.

Ananias went to Saul and put his hands over Saul's eyes. Suddenly Saul could see again.

Saul was baptised a Christian and was given the new name of Paul. He started to tell everyone about Jesus and people who listened to him believed and became Christians too.

Paul has a narrow escape

For three years Paul lived in Damascus, so many people started to believe in Jesus after hearing Paul speak.

However, some people who did not believe that Jesus was sent by God decided they would kill Paul to stop him speaking about Jesus.

They searched for Paul and were watching the city gates so that he could not leave, but some Christians helped Paul by putting him into a basket and lowering him over the city walls with a rope so that he could escape being caught and killed.

Paul goes to Jerusalem

Paul escaped from Damascus and went to Jerusalem to meet with the disciples of Jesus. But when he arrived they were afraid of him because they remembered the days when he was called Saul and persecuted Christians.

One of the disciples, called Barnabas, persuaded them that Paul had changed and had become a good Christian. So Paul started telling people in Jerusalem about Jesus and was so good in his teaching that many people believed him.

This made some people in Jerusalem angry and so they decided to try to kill Paul, but once again he managed to escape with the help of the Christians there.

Paul and Barnabas travel to Cyprus

 Paul and Barnabas started to travel to different countries and cities to tell people about Jesus. Paul started in his home city of Tarsus. He then travelled with Barnabas to the city of Antioch.

After a year there they both travelled to the island of Cyprus and taught people about Jesus in the city of Salamis.

Paul and Barnabas taught the Jewish people in all of the towns and cities they went to. They also taught the gentiles – the non-Jewish people – about Jesus. Even the Governor of Cyprus believed and became a Christian.

More journeys, a miracle and another escape

After Cyprus, Paul and Barnabas went to Perga. They were so successful in having many people believe that some people, jealous of their success, stirred up trouble and

had Paul and Barnabas thrown out of
the area.
After this they went to Lystra where
Paul performed his first miracle and
cured a lame man.

Paul ends up in prison

Paul left Lystra with his friend Silas, and went to a town called Philippi.

When they arrived there they met a slave girl who was a fortune-teller. The girl realised that Paul and his friends were God's messengers and called out to them. Paul told the evil spirit to leave the slave girl. It did, but her masters were angry because she could not tell fortunes any more.

Paul and his friends were brought before a court accused of causing trouble. They were whipped and put into prison.

The earthquake in Philippi

That night in prison, when Paul and his friends were praying, there was a mighty earthquake. The doors to the prison broke open and the prisoners' chains fell off them. The jailer ran to see if the prisoners had escaped but they were all there listening to Paul telling them about Jesus. The other prisoners, and even the jailer, became Christian and the next day Paul and his friends were released.

Paul in Greece

Paul and his friends then travelled to Athens in Greece, a city filled with very wise and clever people. Although many of them there laughed at Paul there were also many who believed what he had to say about Jesus. They too became Christians.

Paul left Athens and went to the city of Corinth. He stayed there for a year and a half, working as a tentmaker and telling people all about Jesus.

Sometimes people would not listen to him and he became sad and discouraged but one night Jesus came to him and told him to have courage because many people did believe what he was telling them.

Paul in Ephesus

Paul eventually left Corinth and headed for Ephesus where he taught more people about Jesus. Many people became Christians and stopped buying silver statues to the goddess Artemis at the temple in the city. The silversmiths started a riot because they were losing money.

However, a good man calmed the riot down so that Paul and his friends were able to leave in peace.

A miracle in Troas

One evening Paul was telling stories about Jesus to a group of people. A young boy who was listening by the window, fell asleep, leaned against the window and fell to the ground.

When they found the boy on the ground he seemed to be dead but Paul picked him up saying: "There is life in him!" and the boy opened his eyes, alive.

Return to Jerusalem

Paul started travelling back to
Jerusalem by boat, stopping at various
places on the way. When he reached
Jerusalem Paul went to the temple,
which was the most important
place in the whole city. Some
people who did not believe
in Jesus started a riot and
dragged Paul out of the
temple. The riot got so bad
that Roman soldiers came
and arrested him.

The next day Paul was taken to the court and he explained how he became a Christian, but the people were so angry that they started rioting again. Paul was taken back to the prison. The Jewish leaders were so angry with Paul because they did not believe what he said and they wanted to kill him. That night Paul had a vision in which Jesus told him to go to Rome.

Paul on trial

Paul's enemies wanted to put him on trial for causing riots. Paul asked that his judge be the Roman Emperor, not the people in Jerusalem who hated him.

He was brought before the Roman Governor, who could not really find anything wrong in what Paul was saying, and he kept Paul in prison because he did not want to upset the leaders in Jerusalem. He did not want another riot so he sent Paul to the King. The King listened to what Paul had to say and thought that he should not be put to death. He almost believed in Paul enough to become a Christian himself. Although he thought Paul ought to be freed, since Paul had asked to be judged by the Roman Emperor they could not free him, Paul had to go to Rome for trial by the Emperor.

Paul is Shipwrecked

Paul was put on a boat to Rome with some other prisoners but on the journey a hurricane struck the boat. The storm went on for days and everyone on board feared they would drown. Paul gave them courage and said that although the boat would be lost they would all be safe. The boat ran aground and started to break up but all on the boat were saved and made it to shore on the island of Malta.

The snake in Malta

The local people in Malta were kind to the shipwrecked survivors but were worried that they were prisoners and might be bad men. While sitting at the fire a snake crawled over Paul's hand and bit him.

The people thought that he would die but when he suffered no harm they realised that he was a special man, blessed by God. They knew this even more when Paul cured a very sick man of a fever on the island.

Paul arrives in Rome

After three months
in Malta Paul went to
Rome where he spent
two years under arrest
in a house. During that
time many people came
to see him to learn about
Jesus. Finally he was
released and allowed to
continue his journeys.

Paul travelled back to many of the
places he had visited before, to
encourage the Christians to live
by the teachings of Jesus. He
wrote many letters to help them
understand how they should live
their lives as Christians.

Paul becomes a martyr

When he reached Rome there was a new Emperor called Nero. Nero blamed the Christians when there was a big fire that burned most of the city. Therefore he decided that all Christians would be arrested and killed, so Paul found himself in prison again.

Paul was put on trial for being a Christian and he was sentenced to death by execution. Paul died in Rome around the year 69 AD but his message about Jesus has been passed on from the many places he visited. We can still read the letters he wrote to the people in these places, which help us today to live our lives as good Christians, and become, like Paul, a friend of Jesus.

How was Stephen killed?

people threw stones.

Who spoke to Saul when he
was riding to Damascus?

Jesus spoke to Saul.

Who helped Paul escape from Damascus?

some christian friends helped Paul.

Who travelled with Paul to Cyprus?

_pa_ _l_ _a__ _d_ _barnbb_ _a_

Name some places they visited.

_Thr__ga_

_____

When Paul became sad and
discouraged who came to him
during the night?

Jesus _came_ _to_
him

When their boat broke up
where did Paul and the other
prisoners end up?

_____

When and where did Paul die?

_____
_____
_____